THE QUEST for GOD

LEONG KWOK THYE

WESTBOW
PRESS®
A DIVISION OF THOMAS NELSON
& ZONDERVAN

THE HOLY BIBLE, NEW INTERNATIONAL VERSION®, NIV® Copyright © 1973, 1978, 1984, 2011 by Biblica, Inc.® Used by permission. All rights reserved worldwide.

WestBow Press books may be ordered through booksellers or by contacting:

WestBow Press
A Division of Thomas Nelson & Zondervan
1663 Liberty Drive
Bloomington, IN 47403
www.westbowpress.com
1 (866) 928-1240

ISBN: 978-1-9736-1210-0 (sc)
ISBN: 978-1-9736-1211-7 (e)

Library of Congress Control Number: 2017919641

Print information available on the last page.

WestBow Press rev. date: 07/26/2019

FOREWORD

"Lord Jesus, we rejoice at your birth,
For in you alone is peace on earth.
We present ourselves an offering
To you, our Saviour, God and King."

This is an example of Kwok Thye's simple but beautiful poems. By connecting every poem here with Bible passage, his poems provide fresh angles with which to reflect in familiar Bible passages. The final stanza in each poem usually offers us a prayer of response to his modern poetic-re-statement of ancient Bible verses.

Thank you, Kwok Thye, for this beautiful collection of Bible Poems.

Rev. Dr. Gordon Wong
President
Trinity Annual Conference
The Methodist Church in Singapore

INTRODUCTION

From the dawn of civilization, man has been earnestly seeking God; what He is like and how to please Him. The need to know God is often driven by fear of the unknown, in particular of death and how eternity will be spent - in heaven or in hell. Philosophers and religious teachers have offered theories of God to assuage anxiety and fear.

The aim of this collection of poems is to present insights of God from a Biblical perspective. God has declared in Isaiah 55:6-8,

> "⁶Seek the Lord while he may be found; call on him while he is near. ⁷Let the wicked forsake his way and the evil man his thoughts. Let him turn to the Lord, and he will abundantly pardon. ⁸For my thoughts are not your thoughts, neither are your ways, my ways."

The Lord's declaration is clear.

> Firstly, he is Creator and God.
> Secondly, he is holy but not inaccessible. Our wickedness has blinded us to him.
> Finally, he is gracious. When we forsake wickedness to seek him, he will pardon us and reveal his thoughts and ways to us.

Knowing God is more than an exercise to assuage fear or to satisfy intellectual curiosity. Search the Scriptures. Allow truths that God will reveal to you to transform your life. In doing so you enter into a vibrant relationship with the living God. More importantly, you will enjoy life with him in eternity.

Leong Kwok Thye

Note.
All Bible texts quoted are from the New International Version.

CONTENTS

¹O Lord, our Lord,
how majestic is your name in all the earth!
³ When I consider your heavens,
the work of your fingers, ...
⁴ What is man that ..... you care for him?
Psalm 8:1-4

A Great and Gracious God

The heavens Lord, declare your glory,
The earth proclaims your majesty!
We marvel at your wondrous grace,
For an insignificant human race.

You form us from the dust of earth,
You give us life by power of your breath.
You make us your own children,
Little lower than the beings in heaven.

You protect infants from danger,
You silence the foe and the avenger.
You lavish us with constant care,
And endless love beyond compare.

You crown us with glory and honour,
And bestow on us your favour
To rule over beasts and birds of the air,
Fish and sea creatures everywhere.

The universe declares your glory,
Creation affirms your sovereignty.
With all nature in one accord,
We praise your majestic name O Lord!

^{27}So God created man in his own image …..
Genesis 1:27

^{7}the Lord God ….. breathed into his nostrils the breath of life,
and the man became a living being.
Genesis 2:7

Man In The Image Of God

The Lord created the universe,
And plants and animals diverse.
He set the stars in space,
Then created the human race.

He formed man from the dust of earth,
And lovingly with his breath,
Made him a living being,
With mind, heart and feeling.

He made man in his own image,
The earth to enjoy and manage;
And made the world a treasure,
For his exclusive pleasure.

He gave him freedom of choice,
To listen and obey his voice:
To walk with him in humility,
And enjoy life into eternity.

But good and evil is God's domain,
Not a function of the brain.
He decides what's good or evil;
Not man, and not the devil.

¹Now the serpent was more crafty than
any of the wild animals …..
He said to the woman, "Did God really say, ….."
Genesis 3:1

⁶ When the woman saw that
the fruit of the tree was good for food…..
she took some and ate it.
She also gave some to her husband, …..and he ate it.
Genesis 3:6

Paradise Lost

The devil being very crafty,
Came to Adam and Eve deceitfully.
He came as a friendly snake,
Dishing advice for Eve's sake,
"The forbidden fruit is good;
It's nutritious and delicious food!"

Eve responded smugly in reply,
"Eat or touch and we will die;
Sneaky snake, you have no clue,
The forbidden fruit is taboo;
God has decreed, we must obey,
It is not what you think or say."

"Goodness, Eve you aren't bright,
You have a misguided insight!
Listen carefully and mark my word,
Eat and you will be wise as God.
It's an opportunity you can't miss
To attain wisdom and eternal bliss."

Eve pondered as she looked,
And finally, she got hooked.
The fruit was pleasant to the eyes,
And eating would make her wise.
So she took the fruit and ate,
As did Adam, her careless mate.

⁹*But the Lord God called to the man, "Where are you?"*
¹⁰ *….. "I heard you …..*
and I was afraid ….. so I hid."
¹¹ *….. "Who told you that you were naked?*
Have you eaten from the tree
from which I commanded you not to eat?"
Genesis 3:9-11

The Lord Intervenes

Sin had led Adam and Eve astray;
So God sought Adam in the cool of day,
"Adam, where are you?" he called.
Adam, alarmed and appalled,
In fear and shame confessed,
"Sorry God, we are undressed."

"Adam, you've been up to no good,
You ate the forbidden food!"
"It was the woman you gave to me,
Gullible and greedy as can be.
She fell for the devil's snare,
Alas, I was caught unaware."

Eve heaved an exasperated sigh,
And argued defensively in reply,
"God, you allowed it to happen;
You put the snake in the garden!
I was not evil or rebellious,
But the fruit looked delicious."

"All I wanted was to get high,
Thank goodness we did not die!
Anyway, it was a silly command,
And one I could not understand.
But I knew you would forgive,
Your goodness would let us live."

¹⁴So the Lord said to the serpent,.....
¹⁵ And I will put enmity…..
between your offspring and hers;…..
¹⁶To the woman he said,
"I will greatly increase
your pains in childbearing; …...
¹⁷To Adam he said, …...
¹⁹"….. for dust you are and
to dust you will return."
Genesis 3:14-19

Not All Is Lost

The Lord gave his verdict clearly
To the parties he found guilty,
"Snake, you are condemned eternally,
To eat dust and crawl on your belly;
For this is your lasting destiny,
In turning mankind against me."

"Henceforth, there will be enmity
Between you and Eve perpetually.
You will cause her offspring pain,
But your scheme will be in vain;
For he will have the authority,
To destroy you completely."

"Eve, in the days that follow;
You will have much sorrow;
You shall long for love and ecstasy,
But childbirth will be agony,
And because you disobeyed me,
You will be under Adam's authority."

"Adam, by listening to your wife;
You will labor hard to survive.
The land you till will not yield,
For I have cursed the field.
From dust you were made,
And to dust you will degrade.

²….. "Repent, for the kingdom of heaven is near."
Matthew 3:2

³"….. make straight in the wilderness
a highway for our God."
⁵And the glory of the Lord will be revealed. …..
Isaiah 40:3-5

The Almighty God Will Come

A voice calling in the wilderness
To a people in helplessness,
"Prepare the way for God Almighty
To come and set his people free."

He will pardon and recompense
His punishment for their offense.
The promise will not be broken;
The mouth of the Lord has spoken.

Every valley shall be raised,
And every mountain razed;
For the long-awaited coming
Of the great and glorious King.

His grace and glory will be revealed;
His people restored and healed.
Like a shepherd he will tenderly
Lead his flock from harm to security.

The Almighty God made everything;
Nations and people are nothing.
None can fathom his understanding,
And none can perceive its meaning.

He sits enthroned above the earth
To give the meek and weary breath,
To soar above their frailty
To be with him in eternity.

⁶For to us a child is born, to us a son is given,
and the government will be on his shoulders.
And he will be called Wonderful Counsellor,
Mighty God, Everlasting Father, Prince of Peace.
Isaiah 9:6

²But for you who revere my name,
the sun of righteousness will rise
with healing in its wings. …..
Malachi 4:2

To Us A Son Is Given

No more gloom and distress,
For those walking in darkness
For to us a Child is given,
God's beloved Son from heaven.

His glorious light will shine,
Indistinguishable and divine.
To bless and enlarge the nation,
And increase our jubilation.

Mighty God, Everlasting Father,
Prince of Peace, Wonderful Counsellor;
His government and peace will increase,
And his blessings will not cease.

By his just and righteous reign,
The kingdom of David will remain;
From thenceforth into eternity,
Established by the Lord Almighty.

The sun of righteousness will arise,
To remove blindness from our eyes;
And the healing in its wings,
Will trample down evil beings.

Freed from the dread of night
By the grace of Jesus' life and light;
We will have life abundantly,
From henceforth into eternity.

⁴So Joseph also went ….. to Bethlehem …..
⁵He went ….. with Mary …..
⁶While they were there, …..
⁷ ….. she gave birth to her firstborn, a son. …..
¹³Suddenly a great company of
the heavenly host appeared
with the angel praising God …..
¹⁴"Glory to God in the highest,
and on earth peace to men on
whom his favour rests."
Luke 2:4-7,13-14

A Saviour Is Born

Joseph travelled to Bethlehem,
A small town close to Jerusalem;
The birthplace of his forefather,
King David, Israel's greatest leader.

With Mary, a virgin bearing a Son;
The Messiah, the Anointed One
Whom God would send to earth,
To save man from sin and death.

Bethlehem was a hive of activity.
None of the inns had vacancy;
Except one with space available
With cows and sheep in a stable.

There, Jesus was born a stranger,
Clothed and bedded in a manger.
King Herod was caught unaware,
The religious leaders didn't care.

But shepherds in a field at night
Were awakened to a glorious sight;
As angels proclaimed the Messiah's birth,
"Peace and goodwill to men on earth".

Lord Jesus, we rejoice at your birth,
For in you alone is peace on earth.
We present ourselves an offering
To you, Saviour, God and King.

¹In the beginning was the Word,
and the Word was with God,
and the Word was God.
⁴In him was life,
and that life was the light of men.
¹⁴The Word became flesh
and made his dwelling among us. .....
John 1:1,4,14

A Wonderful Word

Jesus Christ the eternal Word,
Creator and Triune God,
Came as Son of God incarnate,
To save humanity from its fate.

He came that all may see
God in his grace, truth and glory.
He came to die that all can claim
Salvation in his righteous name.

But the blinded world failed to see,
That the Father's plan in eternity,
Was for Jesus to give life and light,
To humanity groping in the night.

Now everyone who believes,
And everyone who receives
Jesus has the inalienable right,
To be children in God's sight.

Jesus, by offering life and light,
Has freed us from our plight.
It's an act not of man's accord,
But a gift from a loving God.

⁷Jesus said to the servants,
"Fill the jars with water";
so they filled them to the brim.
⁹and the master of the banquet tasted
the water that had been turned into wine. …..
John 2:7-9

²"The kingdom of heaven is like a king
who prepared a wedding banquet for his son.
Matthew 22:2

Invitation To A Wedding Banquet

Jesus accepted an invitation
To a wedding celebration.
The wine pots soon got empty;
Leaving guests still thirsty.

Obedient, he could not resist
His mother's request to assist.
So he turned water into wine;
In his first miraculous sign.

The miracle shows his authority
Over distress and calamity.
The sign directs attention
To God's plan of salvation.

God invites all, even the least
To his Son's wedding feast.
All who accept the invitation,
Will receive his salvation.

He will change them in design,
As Jesus changed water into wine;
They will drink wine that satisfy;
New wine that does not run dry.

*⁵ "….. no-one can enter the kingdom of God
unless he is born of water and the Spirit.
⁷….. 'You must be born again.'
⁸The wind blows wherever it pleases. …..
So it is with everyone born of the Spirit."
John 3:5-8*

Into The Kingdom Of God

God longs to give you freedom
To enter into his Kingdom.
He will empower and enable
You to be his special people.

He will cleanse your impurity,
And free you from idolatry,
Your spirit and soul renew,
If you allow him to change you.

From whence the wind blows,
To where it goes, no one knows.
But when the trees are swaying,
You know the wind is blowing.

Thus when you have a longing,
It's his Spirit that is working.
Cease from striving and sin.
And you will have peace within,

For you will be born anew;
As he has promised you,
And have complete freedom,
To enter into his kingdom.

⁵Simon answered,
"Master, we've worked hard all night
and haven't caught anything. …..
⁶When they had done so,
they caught such a large number of fish …..
¹⁰…..Then Jesus said to Simon,
"Don't be afraid;
from now on you will catch men."
Luke 5:5-10

A Great Harvest With Jesus

Peter, Andrew, James and John,
Had fished from dusk till dawn.
Their labour had been frustrating;
They did not catch anything.

Jesus was teaching that morning.
So when the crowd kept increasing,
He stepped into Peter's boat,
Then cleaned, idle and afloat.

When Jesus had finished teaching,
And the crowd began dispersing,
He told an exhausted Peter,
"Cast your net in deep water."

Peter had a great catch of fish
Far more than his wildest wish.
In response to his frantic cue,
James and John came to the rescue.

Peter, bowing down at Jesus' knees
Said, "Lord, depart from me please,
For I am sinful and unworthy,
To be in your hallowed company."

Jesus looked kindly at him said,
"Simon Peter, do no be afraid,
I will be with you to enable
You henceforth to fish for people."

[10] *Jesus said, "Make the people sit down."*
….. the men sat down, about five thousand of them.
[12] When they had all had enough to eat,
he said to his disciples,
"Gather the pieces that are left over.
Let nothing be wasted."
John 6:10-12

Five Loaves And Two Small Fish

The hungry crowd needed to be fed.
"Philip, where can we buy bread?"
Jesus' intention was to set a test,
But Philip responded in protest.

Then Andrew found a little lad,
Willing to give Jesus all he had;
Two small fish and five loaves of bread,
That the hungry crowd be fed.

Jesus gave thanks for the food,
And blessed it for the common good.
After all had eaten their fill,
There was plenty leftovers still.

A meager meal of fish and bread,
And five thousand persons were fed.
Jesus will graciously multiply,
Whatever we willing supply.

What we have does not matter,
Jesus can always make it better.
A task may seem impossible;
With God all things are possible.

⁴⁰ A man with leprosy came to him
and begged him on his knees, …..
⁴¹ Filled with compassion,
Jesus reached out his hand and touched the man. …..
⁴² Immediately the leprosy left him and he was cured.
Mark 1:40-42

A Touch Of Love

The leper longed for release,
From a body ravaged by disease.
He came to Jesus with a plea,
"Set my imprisoned being free."

Jesus could heal him from a distance,
But the leper longed for his presence;
For not only the body but the soul,
Needed to be made whole.

He touched the leper with his hand,
The disease left at his command.
An act unpleasant by any measure,
But a gesture the leper would treasure.

For no longer despised and rejected,
He was loved and accepted
By no other than the Son of God;
His wonderful Saviour and Lord,

Lord, we are your heart and hands,
To carry out your commands.
Help us to show the love of Jesus.
Under demanding circumstances,

You love the despised, Lord Jesus,
As much as you love us.
You can touch the wounded soul,
To heal and make him whole.

⁵Jesus loved Martha and her sister and Lazarus.
⁶Yet ….. he stayed where he was two more days.
²⁵Jesus said to her,
"I am the resurrection and the life.
He who believes in me will live,
even thought he dies;
²⁶and whoever lives and believes in me
will never die. …..
John 11:5-6,25-26

²²For as in Adam all die,
so in Christ all will be made alive.
1 Corinthians 15:22

Dying To Live

Mary and Martha made a plea,
Appealing to Jesus' mercy.
Their brother Lazarus was dying,
But Jesus kept on delaying.

No one knew the reason why
Jesus allowed Lazarus to die.
Till at the grave with the family,
He showed his love and authority

Much to every one's surprise,
He caused dead Lazarus to rise,
"He who lives and believes in me
Shall not die but live eternally."

Man like grass in the morning,
Will surely die by evening.
We have a life span of seventy;
And if strong, perhaps eighty.

For as in Adam death will reign,
So in Christ we will rise again;
For he has secured victory,
Over death and mortality.

³Now this is eternal life:
that they may know you,
the only true God,
and Jesus Christ whom you have sent.
John 17:3

⁸Taste and see
that the Lord is good;
blessed is the man
who takes refuge in him.
Psalm 34:8

Eternal Life

There is none righteous, not one;
Only God's beloved perfect Son.
We need his righteousness,
In our pursuit of holiness.

Eternal life is to know God,
By receiving Jesus Christ as Lord.
To be freed from death and sin,
And have peace and power within.

Eternal life begins on earth,
From outset of spiritual birth;
To walk with the Lord Almighty,
From thenceforth into eternity.

To know God not as an illusion,
Based on a shifting foundation;
Not a quest for an elusive goal,
To assuage the thirsty soul.

It is a foretaste of heaven,
As God's beloved children;
Knowing beyond fear and sorrow,
That there is a bright tomorrow.

*[18]Here they crucified him,
and with him two others …....
John 19:18*

*[5]But he was pierced for our transgressions,
he was crushed for our iniquities;
the punishment that brought us peace
was upon him, and by his wounds
we are healed.
Isaiah 53:5*

Jesus Christ Was Crucified

Jesus Christ was crucified;
In agony and pain he died.
Not for wrongs he had done,
But because he was God's Son.

Like sheep we have all gone astray,
Each one to his own wicked way.
So God ordained his suffering
As our guilt and sin offering.

He took on our infirmities,
Was crushed for our iniquities;
A righteous God to appease,
Our bondage in sin to release.

He lived to serve and forgive,
And died that we might live;
To bring us as God's children,
Into the kingdom of heaven.

Jesus heals the wounded soul;
Restores and makes it whole,
Reconciles us to a loving God
By shedding his precious blood.

His love is without reserve,
Redeeming love we don't deserve.
Grant us a heart of thankfulness,
O Lord, for your great faithfulness.

¹On the first day of the week, …..
the women….. went to the tomb.
⁴ ….. suddenly two men ….. stood beside them.
⁶He is not here; he has risen! …..
⁷'The Son of Man must ….. be crucified and
on the third day be raised again.' "
Luke 24:1-7

Jesus Christ Is Risen!

Early on the first Easter morn,
When all hope seems to have gone;
The women took spices to the grave,
Of the Messiah God did not save.

The sealed tomb was wide open!
How on earth did this happen?
Inside, it was clearly empty,
Where was the Messiah's body?

Suddenly, without any warning,
Two men dressed like lightning;
Calmed the women and said,
"Why seek the living among the dead?"

Then Jesus showed his risen body,
For his followers to touch and see;
To continue the task he had begun
As the Father's Anointed Son.

The prophets had prophesied;
The Messiah must be crucified.
But his death will not be in vain,
On the third day he will rise again.

Jesus' resurrected body
Is now no longer a mystery.
Invite him to dwell in you;
To revive and make you new.

⁷He said to them:
"It is not for you to know the times or dates
the Father has set by his own authority.
⁸But you will receive power
when the Holy Spirit comes on you;
and you will be my witnesses
in Jerusalem, and in all Judea and Samaria,
and to the ends of the earth."
Acts 1:7-8

Mission Accomplished

Jesus by his resurrection;
Secured God's plan for salvation.
He has achieved final victory,
Over sin, death and mortality.

He gave his apostles clear proof,
And told them to declare the truth
The doubting world needed to hear,
That the kingdom of God is near.

He promised they would inherit
The gift of the Holy Spirit,
Who would ever be by their side
To comfort, empower and guide.

They should continue the mission,
Of his Father's great commission
To battle sin and unrighteousness,
And lead the world to holiness.

Our task is to spread the word,
That our Saviour, Lord and God
Will soon come to earth again;
In glory forever to reign.

*42"Therefore keep watch,
because you do not know
on what day your Lord will come.
Matthew 24:42*

*31"When the Son of Man comes in his glory, …..
32…. he will separate the people
one from another as a shepherd
separates the sheep from the goats.
Matthew 25:31-32*

Jesus Christ Will Come Again

Jesus Christ will come again as King;
As Lord of the dead and living
To separate the wicked and righteous,
On basis of their faithfulness.

The downtrodden are his proxy,
For us to extend grace and mercy;
And the blessings that we share,
Is evidence of his love and care.

Those who serve him faithfully,
He will reward in eternity.
Those who chose to live selfishly,
He will punish accordingly.

When he comes, we do not know -
Beyond our lifetime or tomorrow?
But we must be always ready,
As he will return suddenly.

Lord, may our life be a fragrance
Lived daily in your presence;
May every deed be an offering,
To you, righteous Judge and King.

*⁶With what shall I come before the Lord .....?
with burnt offerings .....? ⁷..... with thousands of rams .....?
Shall I offer my firstborn for my transgression .....?
⁸ ..... And what does the Lord require of you?
To act justly and to love mercy
and to walk humbly with your God.
Micah 6:6-8*

What Shall I Offer To The Lord?

How shall I come before the Lord,
Bow down before the exalted God?
Will a perfect prescribed sacrifice
Offered on the altar suffice?

Will sacrifices in abundance
Offered without repentance,
Will the gift of my firstborn alone,
My life transform, my sin atone?

You have shown, Lord, what is right
In your sovereign righteous sight;
Walk before the Lord Almighty,
And submit to him in humility.

Show justice, love and mercy
To the oppressed and the needy.
Lord, melt my hardened heart aflame,
To bless others in your name.

13 "You are the salt of the earth. .....
14"You are the light of the world. .....
Matthew 5:13-14

3"For God so loved the world
that he gave his one and only Son,
that whoever believes in him
shall not perish but have eternal life.
John 3:16

Hearts and Hands for Jesus

Touch us O Lord, cause us to see,
The needs within our community;
That those in anguish and despair,
May know you, Lord, because we care.

Mould us O Lord, that we may be,
Your heart and hands for humanity;
That all who taste your goodness, Lord,
May find in you a loving God.

Infuse us Lord, with Jesus' love,
That when you call us, we will move;
For you have sent your Son to give
His precious life that all might live.

Inspire us Lord, set hearts aflame,
In zealous honor of your name;
That with all creation in one accord,
We acclaim you as its Lord and God.

*⁸Do not let this Book of the Law
depart from your mouth; …..
Then you will be prosperous and successful.
⁹ ….. Do not be terrified;
do not be discouraged,
for the Lord your God
will be with you wherever you go."
Joshua 1:8-9*

The Journey Of Life

We journey through the unknown,
To a home we have yet to own;
A wonderful home in eternity,
Promised by the Lord Almighty.

It is a challenging journey,
Often through hostile territory.
But God will be with us all the way
If we obey him night and day.

When the path ahead looks dim,
We need to walk close to him.
For the Guardian of our soul,
Is sovereign and in control.

When storms arise and rage,
He gives strength and courage.
When forces of evil assail,
His faithfulness does not fail.

We should not be terrified,
For the Lord is ever by our side;
To guide, to protect and to bless
Us with prosperity and success.

4Jesus answered:
"Watch out that no one deceives you.
5For many will come in my name,
claiming, 'I am the Christ,'.....
13but he who stands firm
to the end will be saved.
14And this gospel .....
will be preached in the whole world .....
then the end will come.
Matthew 24:4-5,13-14

The End of the Age

The disciples asked Jesus privately,
"Lord, when will these things be?
Give us a sign visible and clear,
That the end of the age is here."

Jesus replied with a precaution,
To forestall their speculation,
"Many false prophets will claim
That they come in my name."

"You will be severely tested,
Persecuted and executed.
Hold to truths you have received.
Do not doubt and be deceived."

"There will be global calamities,
And cosmic catastrophes.
Birth pains the world will bear,
Is the sign my return is near."

"Do not let your love grow cold,
Be faithful, steadfast and bold.
Preach the gospel in every domain,
Then I will return to earth again."

²I saw the Holy City, the new Jerusalem,
coming down out of heaven from God, …..
³ And I heard a loud voice
from the throne saying,
"Now the dwelling of God is with men, …..
²⁷Nothing impure will ever enter it,
….. only those whose names
are written in the Lamb's book of life.
Revelation 21: 2-3, 27

The City of God

The first heaven and earth will pass away,
A new heaven and earth will come to stay;
The new Jerusalem, the Holy City;
Will descend from heaven in beauty.

We will be with God as his people
To enjoy a life imperishable.
There will be no death or mourning,
Neither will there be pain or crying.

The city does not need external light,
For never again will there be night,.
The Lamb is the lamp and God the glory,
Of this majestic celestial city.

There is no visible temple in the city;
Its temple is the Lamb and God Almighty;
Kings in splendor and nations will delight
To walk humbly by its glorious light.

The city gates will never be shut,
But impurity and evil will be kept out;
All in the Lamb's book of life will enter,
To dwell with the Lord God forever.

ABOUT THE AUTHOR

The author is a Chartered Civil Engineer. He developed a passion for Bible study and Christian literature during his student days in Australia through the Overseas Christian Fellowship, a student movement affiliated to the Inter-Varsity Fellowship.

He continued this passion on his return to Singapore through Scripture Union, the Christian Book Centre, and the Bible Study Fellowship. He has also been involved in facilitating development of Bible study groups for adults and pastoral care ministries for students. He reads widely for leisure and to keep abreast of current affairs.

Printed in the United States
By Bookmasters